Abraham

ADVENTURES OF FAITH

CWR

Dave Edwins

Contents

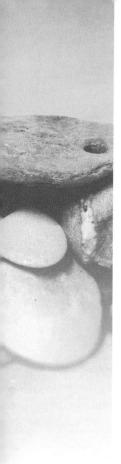

Introduction

During the troubled times of the seventeenth century, when civil war raged in the British Isles, Parliamentarians, commonly called Roundheads, fought with those loyal to King Charles I (Royalists) and eventually captured him, brought him to trial and executed him in 1649. That same year Oliver Cromwell, leader of the Parliamentarians, commissioned Samuel Cooper, a renowned portrait painter of the time, to paint him. The challenge was that Cooper was to paint Cromwell, 'warts and all!' The portrait of Abraham drawn in Genesis has a similar feel because it contains many blemishes as well as evidence of his tenacious faith. He is no plastic saint but a real live human being, who was prone to make mistakes just like us.

Abraham's father Terah, a descendent of Noah's son Shem, lived near Ur, a busy commercial centre in Mesopotamia close to where the Euphrates River met the Persian Gulf (modern-day Iraq). The city was dominated by a huge temple Ziggurat devoted to Nanna, the Moon God, and many in this pagan city indulged in worship ceremonies that were grossly impure. According to Joshua 24:15, Terah's family had also been caught up with worshipping other gods. For some reason Terah decides to take the whole family to the north to a place called Harran (this spelling was common at the time and it separates it from the name of Terah's other son, Haran) in Genesis 11:31. Perhaps God had already spoken to Abraham in Ur and called him to follow wherever He would lead him, and Terah was simply putting off the inevitable separation from his son for a future time.

Terah's family were shepherds, probably quite wealthy, and it also appears that Abraham had prospered whilst in Harran (Gen. 12:5). Quite how the revelation of God came to Abraham we are not told in the text, but it was obviously a strong calling that convinced him to be obedient.

Accompanying the calling were key promises made by God concerning giving him a land, descendants and blessing which would spill over to others. I will call him Abraham throughout for continuity's sake, for when God appeared to him to ratify the covenant in Genesis 17, and instituted the rite of circumcision, God changed his name from Abram to Abraham: no longer 'high father' or 'exalted father' but from then onwards 'Father of many nations.' Also at that time God changed his wife Sarai's name to an updated form, Sarah, 'noble woman' or 'princess', for she too was part of this covenant that God forged with Abraham, and would be the mother of nations and of kings. Abraham's submission to God and his willingness to cut across the conventions of his time challenges us as we seek to be true disciples. Hearing God and living in obedience to Him takes courage and faith, especially in a twenty-first century world that is sceptical and secular in its outlook.

The New Testament often refers back to Abraham as an example of what believing God is all about; see Romans 4 where Paul develops this discussion. Abraham was made right with God not by obedience to the Law but by exercising faith in God's promises. Later in the story of Abraham we will see how he demonstrated that faith by trusting that Isaac would even be raised from the dead in Genesis 22. The writer to the Hebrews, in the famous heroes of the faith in chapter 11, devotes more verses to Abraham than any other person mentioned, because he was chosen by God to be 'the channel through which God would work to reach the world with the message of salvation'.* Through Abraham and his family, God intended to demonstrate His love and mercy to a wider world. The role of the nation of Israel was to make visible the relational love of God and His glory (beauty) so that people looking on would respond in faith (Ezek. 16:14). This task is now to be undertaken by the Church, due to the constant unfaithfulness of His ancient people Israel. The choice of Abraham was not arbitrary or made out of personal

*G.A. Getz, *Abraham – Trials and Triumphs* (Glendale, CA; Regal, 1979, p12).

favouritism; Abraham and his family had an important assignment sharing the grace and truth of a holy God.

Paul writes to the Galatians (3:6) and says 'Consider Abraham', and that is what these studies are all about, looking at Abraham and learning from his bold faith but also his fearful miscalculations. We will detect a winsome motivation, a desire to please God and a loyal devotion to the One who called him out of paganism to be the leader of a holy people. The principles that emerge from these stories will be important for our own journey of discipleship too. Perhaps the highest accolade given to Abraham in the Bible is that of being a 'friend of God', see 2 Chronicles 20:7, Isaiah 41:8 and James 2:23. Jesus also describes His disciples, just before His betrayal and death, as His friends in John 15:9–17. What an awesome privilege to be called 'Friends of God', for that is what we are!

WEEK 1

Faith and Disobedience
(Genesis 12:1–20)

Opening Icebreaker

Think back to a time when you were fearful about something. What did you do to in order to improve the situation? Share with the group your feelings and work out a strategy for dealing with these kinds of issues in the future. Pray for one another.

Bible Readings

- Genesis 11:27–32
- Genesis 12:1–20
- Galatians 3:6–9
- Acts 26:12–20
- Hebrews 11:8–10

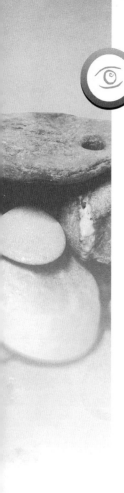

Opening Our Eyes

Leaving behind the comforts of life in Mesopotamia and worship practices that were decidedly immoral, Abraham starts out on his journey of faith. The Bible indicates that he received God's call whilst in Ur and that the move to Harran with his father Terah was just stage one of his steps of obedience (Acts 7:2). We do not know how he encountered God or the details of his change of heart. Abraham was a pioneer and had perhaps only glimpses of truths that we hold dear; that is what makes his story all the more remarkable. Maybe Abraham paused in Harran whilst Terah was still alive, to honour him as sons were supposed to do in that culture. It was certainly an enormous step of faith and massive counter-cultural shift to relocate his considerable family, flocks and herds, and live the life of a semi-nomad. For us, too, discipleship is a journey and it requires that we walk it, trusting the One who called us to follow. There will be stops and starts but the essential requirement is that we remain obedient.

Lot, who was the son of Abraham's brother Haran, also travelled with the family group as they made their way towards the south and the land of Canaan. They travelled as far as Shechem and there they paused whilst Abraham received further instructions from God, plus a confirmation of God's blessing in Genesis 12:7. It is interesting to note that the patriarchs, of whom Abraham was the first, seemed to build altars wherever they went (12:7,8 and see 26:25; 33:20; 35:7). The suggestion is that these altars indicated that Abraham was laying claim to the land that God had promised. God met him there at Shechem in a tangible way and if Abraham had only heard God's voice before, now he met with the living God and would be forever changed. Abraham's family would return to these altars again and again to worship and meet with God (see Gen. 26:23–25; 46:1 for example). Where are the special places in your life where God speaks and you know His presence? Whilst at Moorlands College I used to take students away on retreat to a Franciscan Friary and I was aware that God would frequently speak into my life while I was in that place.

The second half of the chapter reads very differently from the first. If we detect intimacy with God and an obedient walk of faith in verses 1–9, it is quite a different story in verses 10–20. A famine hits the country and Abraham moves his family and flocks down to Egypt. Sensible no doubt in human terms, but did he consult God? Famines don't usually develop overnight! As Abraham enters Egypt, doubts and fear plague his mind, especially regarding his beautiful wife Sarah and how the Egyptians would view her. 'With a brutal disregard for Sarah, and a total lapse from faith in his Lord, Abraham resorted to deceit in order to save his own skin.'* So Sarah is introduced as his sister and while Abraham enjoys fiscal success, Sarah is consigned to Pharaoh's harem. When God intervenes in His mercy, Pharaoh gets the message! Sometimes when we go our own way God steps in to put the problem right even though we do not deserve it. He had a far greater purpose for Abraham and Sarah than perhaps they even dreamed of, and it would not be thwarted!

*J.G. Baldwin, *The Message of Genesis* (Leicester: IVP, 1999) p38.

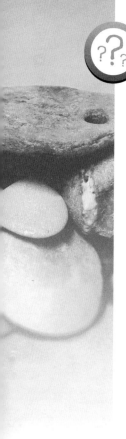

Discussion Starters

1. As you have read the passage in Genesis what particularly stood out for you?

   Mobile ~~[crossed out]~~
   tribes

2. Imagine you are Abraham. How would you tell Sarah that you need to move but you don't know where you are going?

   Worried
   Particular their days

3. Consider the idea that faith is like taking a step forward into a darkened room. Has God ever called you to leave a familiar situation and step out into the unknown?

4. How do we discern God's will for our lives? Share some examples with the group.

5. What are the marker points (your altars) in your discipleship journey that are important for you?

_____

_____

_____

_____

_____

6. What lesson do you think Abraham could learn from God's intervention in Egypt (vv17–20)?

_____

_____

_____

_____

_____

7. Can you think of an occasion when you have been disobedient to God? What were the consequences and how did you grow through the situation and get back on track?

_____

_____

_____

_____

_____

8. What can we learn about God's mercy and care from this story?

_____

_____

_____

_____

_____

Personal Application

The faith that Abraham displayed was not discovered in any textbook but developed through a life where he made numerous mistakes and faced many tough situations. To step out of his comfort zone in Ur and Harran and follow God, not knowing where he was going, demanded great obedience and trust. When we receive Christ as our Saviour, we do it by faith. It is not so much a step into the dark unknown but rather a commitment to a God who has revealed Himself in Christ. From that moment we begin a life of trust and a pilgrimage of hope, and as faith grows we learn to trust Him more. Where are you at this time? To use a swimming analogy, have you taken the plunge like Abraham or are you still dithering on the edge of the pool?

Seeing Jesus in the Scriptures

Abraham is important for us today and is not just the father of the Jewish nation but also, as Christians, our forefather too (Rom. 4:11,18). Told by God that he would be the father of nations he could not have imagined all that it would mean for Christ's followers today. Abraham demonstrated how it is possible for a person to be made right with God through faith and not by works. The Law had not yet been given, so clearly Abraham's right living was not based on that but rather on the conviction of faith. There is a definite foreshadowing of the gospel of the grace of Christ here.

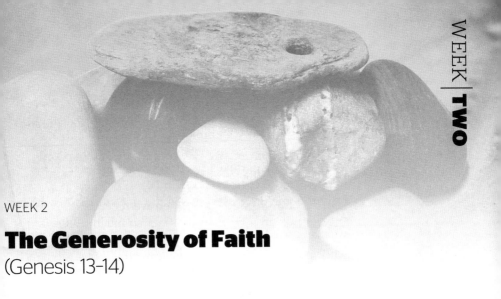

WEEK 2

The Generosity of Faith
(Genesis 13–14)

Opening Icebreaker

As a group think about how you can demonstrate
kindness to someone not expecting it, perhaps a
neighbour who is in real need or a church member who
has hit a rough patch? Be practical and work out how you
can realistically demonstrate God's love together. Steve
Sjogren says, 'As we speak the language of love through
serving, we break down the communication barriers
between the church and the world'.*

Bible Readings

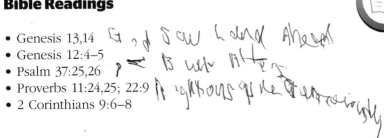

- Genesis 13,14
- Genesis 12:4–5
- Psalm 37:25,26
- Proverbs 11:24,25; 22:9
- 2 Corinthians 9:6–8

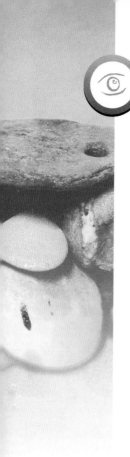

Opening Our Eyes

I have always been intrigued by the fact that Lot, Abraham's nephew, travelled with him from Harran. Was it that Abraham felt a sense of obligation for his dead brother? Did he have a particularly strong relationship with his nephew and feel he could help Lot to develop as a leader? Some have even posed the question as to whether Abraham disobeyed God by taking Lot with him, as he was supposed to leave his country, his people and his father's household (Gen. 12:1)! No doubt Lot would have learned much from his uncle's devotion and faith as they journeyed together to Canaan and then to Egypt. On their return to Canaan, following the debacle in Egypt with Pharaoh, Abraham leads them back to Bethel, where he had already built an altar in Genesis 12:8. When you begin to understand the implications of our wrong decisions, the place to return to is where you began; in Abraham's case, Bethel. We notice that he once again renewed his relationship with God (Gen. 13:4).

The land where Abraham and Lot settled was vast, but the two households stayed close together, perhaps for security reasons. Soon there was trouble brewing between the two sets of herdsmen, due to the fact that they had both prospered! Water rights and good pastureland were in short supply and caused serious issues between them. So Abraham made a sensible suggestion – why not separate and give themselves more room? He then generously offered Lot the choice, the fertile plain near to the Jordan River or the lowland to the west, where the Canaanites lived. Lot could not believe his good fortune and, disregarding his uncle's wellbeing, he selfishly chose the land to the east. The land was indeed fertile, but the choice was also fraught with danger, due to the immorality and violence that was rife in the nearby cities of Sodom and Gomorrah (Gen. 13:13). We also need to be careful in the choices we make in life! Stuart Briscoe comments, 'Abraham knew in his heart that even when the promised land didn't look too promising, the Lord of the promise was faithful, and the correct response to faithfulness is a fullness of faith'.*

Sadly, Lot gets caught up as innocent victim in some intertribal conflict in chapter 13. A group of kings led by Kedorlaomer from Elam attack Sodom and Gomorrah, and Lot and his family are captured. The news reaches Abraham, who is now living at Mamre near Hebron, and his immediate reaction is to lead an expeditionary force of 318 men to free his nephew. Here is generosity of the highest order! Abraham might have been forgiven for thinking: *Lot chose the best land with no thought for me, so let him extricate himself from this tricky situation!* Instead, Abraham defeats Kedorlaomer and his allies in a daring night attack and frees Lot to return home to Sodom.

Look at the incident with Melchizedek in 14:18–20 and try to work out what was going on. We know very little about this mysterious character, except he was King of Salem (Jerusalem) and a priest, who also worshipped Abraham's God. After receiving the nourishment of bread and wine, Abraham gives him a tithe or tenth of his spoils of war. Clearly Melchizedek was his superior, indicated by the offering and the blessing of Abraham. Check out Psalm 110:4, Hebrews 6:20 and 7:2–10. The writer of Hebrews certainly saw Melchizedek as a foreshadowing of our great King and Priest, Jesus.

*S. Briscoe, *Devotions for Men* (Wheaton, IL: Tyndale, 2000) p101.

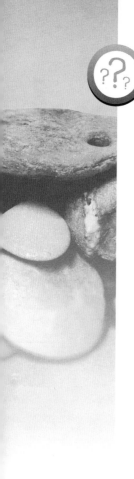

Discussion Starters

1. We know that Abraham was very wealthy when he returned from Egypt. Why does wealth often cause problems for Christians and how can we develop a greater generosity of spirit?

    _____

    _____

    _____

    _____

2. The pain of wrong choices often lingers. If you are able, share with the group how you may have dealt with that in your discipleship journey.

    _____

    _____

    _____

    _____

3. What renewed and developed promises are given to Abraham in Genesis 13:14–17? Why was it important for Abraham to hear these afresh?

    _____

    _____

    _____

    _____

4. Conflict is common in life. What does it mean to be a peacemaker in the world today? Spend time praying for areas of the world where conflict is endemic.

    _____

    _____

    _____

    _____

5. Many people still suffer under the curse of slavery, perhaps in the sex industry or as they are exploited by unscrupulous employers. What can you do to help set people free? Investigate the work of the A21 Campaign, Not For Sale or Hope for Justice

_____

_____

_____

_____

6. Investigate the curious story of Melchizedek in Genesis 14:18–20. The blessing seems to revolve around thanksgiving for the victory just accomplished. How thankful are we for the many blessings of God?

_____

_____

_____

_____

7. There are always a lot of differing views expressed about tithing. Is tithing still valid today? Discuss the whole area of giving, especially as an expression of thankfulness.

_____

_____

_____

_____

8. Why do you think that Abraham refused to keep the spoils of war and refused the generosity of the King of Sodom? Are there lessons for us to learn here?

_____

_____

_____

_____

Personal Application

Generosity shines through chapters 13 and 14. Abraham allows Lot to settle in the best land and then proceeds to rescue his nephew from the captivity of Kedorlaomer. Returning from battle, Abraham is met by the mysterious Melchizedek and is given sustenance of bread and wine. With thanksgiving he responds by offering a tenth of everything he had gained in the battle.

As children of their heavenly Father it is expected that Christians should display a spirit of generosity. The well-known verse John 3:16 declares that 'God so loved the world that He gave' (see also Titus 3:4–7). God's nature is always to be lavish in love and generosity. Consider all He supplies in creation for our blessing and growth, calling us to display a family likeness in Deuteronomy 15:10, Proverbs 11:25 and 22:9, and 2 Corinthians 9:6. So how does this challenge you today? Why not review all aspects of your giving, not only in financial terms.

Seeing Jesus in the Scriptures

Melchizedek is declared to be King of Salem and also a priest of God (Gen. 14:18). The writer to the Hebrews picks up this theme in chapter 7 and likens him to Jesus, our great High Priest. Melchizedek is portrayed as being greater than Levi, father of the priestly tribe, Abraham's great-grandson and a foreshadowing of Jesus (Heb. 7:6,10,15,16). The old sacrificial system, which depended on an earthly priest entering once a year into the Temple to offer an animal sacrifice, has lost its validity because a greater High Priest, Jesus, from the priestly order of Melchizedek, has offered His own life once for all (Heb. 7:27).   •

WEEK 3

Faith for the Future
(Genesis 15–17)

Opening Icebreaker

Give everyone in the group a few small pieces of paper or card, and a pen. Then spend a few minutes thinking about your personal fears. Write each one down on a separate piece and collect them up (maximum of three each!). Work out what are the common fears of the group and pray for God's help to overcome them.

Bible Readings

- Genesis 15–17
- Romans 4
- Acts 7:2–8
- Galatians 3:6–9
- Hebrews 6:13–16

Opening Our Eyes

As Abraham returned from his adventure of rescuing his ungrateful, selfish nephew Lot, he is confronted by a vision from God. It appears that Abraham may have been rattled by the encounter with Kedorlaomer and his four allies, anxious lest his enemies would attack him directly. So God promises him protection, saying 'I am your shield'. Also, having refused the offer of financial remuneration from the King of Sodom, he was given the assurance that God would be his reward (15:1). Meanwhile, Abraham is also concerned about his lack of an heir: ten years have elapsed since the original promise and it seems to him that the only alternative is that a trusted servant would inherit his possessions. God assures him that a son would be born and confirmed it with a lesson from the night sky. Genesis 15:6 is the crucial verse here and the New Testament doctrine of salvation by faith is explained by Paul in Romans 4.

The covenant promise to Abraham is confirmed by the mysterious ceremony in the latter part of chapter 15. It was common practice at that time to have a ritual like this to ratify an agreement (see Jer. 34:18–20). Usually both parties would pass between the divided animal carcasses. However, in this case the symbols of a smoking pot and a blazing torch sufficed, reminding Abraham that it was God who instigated this covenant and would fully complete the terms without Abraham's interference! It would have been good if Sarah had understood this too!

The human side of Abraham emerges once more in chapter 16, with Sarah's frustration at not being able to bear children, suggesting that their family line could be continued by a surrogacy arrangement with her servant Hagar. This venture demonstrates how easy it is after great blessing and exciting encounters with God to default to human effort once again. The pregnant Hagar runs for

her life to avoid further conflict in the household and
mistreatment by Sarah. Running away may alleviate the
immediacy of our problems but never solves them. What
follows is another indication of the grace of God. The
angel of the LORD finds her in the desert by a spring of
water and gives her phenomenal promises concerning her
unborn child. Notice the initial questioning in verse 8,
which enables Hagar to face her fears. We never need fear
the gentle probing of our faithful God. Interestingly, Hagar
discovers a new name for God, 'the One who sees me'.

Abraham has another encounter with God in chapter 17,
but in case we think these were frequent occurrences,
look at the time between them! Some fourteen years have
elapsed since Hagar returned to camp and gave birth to
Ishmael. We love those special times when God manifests
His presence to us but they are never routine and often
come as surprises. Here God refers to Himself as God
Almighty or El Shaddai, the unchanging or immovable
rock, the faithful One who can transform situations that
are humanly impossible. Abraham's reaction in verse 3
is to fall face down to the ground whilst hearing a call
to be blameless. This was not a call to sinless perfection
but rather to give God his wholehearted devotion. This
renewal of the covenant included a confirmation of an
enlarged family, inheritance of the land and the name
change to Abraham, which means 'father of many nations'.
A sign of this renewed covenant was the introduction of
the rite of circumcision.

Discussion Starters

1. Share about times in your lives when you have heard God's gracious words, 'Do not be afraid'.

_____

_____

_____

_____

2. What issue was Abraham most concerned about in chapter 15? What solution did he offer to God? How did God respond?

_____

_____

_____

_____

3. Read Romans 4 and consider how Paul uses Genesis 15:6 to show that a right relationship with God comes only by faith, not by human effort.

_____

_____

_____

_____

4. How would you answer the questions posed to Hagar in Genesis 16:8?

_____

_____

_____

_____

5. Unfulfilled promises and dreams are often difficult for us to handle. How can you minister to people in your church who struggle in these areas?

_____

_____

_____

_____

6. We are faced with many moral and ethical dilemmas today, and surrogacy is just one of them. How can we respond graciously but yet biblically to these tough questions?

_____

_____

_____

_____

7. Have you ever had a powerful experience of meeting with God? Have you been able to share that without appearing spiritually proud? Should we expect these to be normal in our daily walk with God?

_____

_____

_____

_____

8. Read again Genesis 17:17–22 and discuss Abraham's reaction to God's reiterated promises. Here Abraham laughs, listens and questions God: how does this help us in our relationship with our heavenly Father?

_____

_____

_____

_____

Personal Application

Have you ever thought that God was being slow in fulfilling a dream or a promise: perhaps the conversion of a loved one, healing from illness or the opening up of a new job opportunity? Abraham discovered that God was indeed 'El Shaddai', the Almighty One, who would never let him down and would fulfil all His promises. Yet still Abraham felt it necessary to 'help God out' in order to produce a son and heir. There will be many times in our lives when we struggle to believe, and we are plagued with doubt. Remember that doubt is normal and not to be feared, as Frederick Buechner once said, 'Doubts are the ants in the pants of faith. They keep it awake and moving."* God never gives up on Abraham, even when he is unbelieving, because He sees the bigger picture and is committed to him.

Seeing Jesus in the Scriptures

Notice God's care for Hagar in chapter 16, a servant girl caught up in the drama of Abraham's household. Unconsulted in the surrogacy process planned by Sarah, Hagar uses the ensuing pregnancy to hurt her mistress. One can only imagine the fiery exchanges between them and Hagar's satisfaction in rubbing salt into the wound. While running away from the camp, totally alone and vulnerable, Hagar meets God's messenger who challenges her fears and speaks blessing into her life. Who was this 'angel of the LORD'? Some think that it was Jesus pre-incarnate. One thing is certain, that God loved Hagar and her unborn child and had promises for them also. When you are at life's extremity always make room for Jesus to meet you!

*Frederick Buechner, *Wishful Thinking* (HarperCollins: 1973).

WEEK 4

The Prayer of Faith
(Genesis 18-19)

Opening Icebreaker

Gather some quotes from the Bible and internet on prayer.
Print these on small cards and give every member of
the group a quote. Allow a short time for thinking about
the individual quotes and then share with each other the
things you can learn from them.

Bible Readings

- Genesis 18–19
- Matthew 6:5–15
- Matthew 17:14–21
- Mark 5:21–34
- James 5:13–18

Opening Our Eyes

Imagine the scene: Abraham is dozing at the entrance of his tent, it is cooler there out of the glare of the midday sun, when suddenly he notices three strangers nearby. His immediate reaction demonstrates the Bedouin sacred duty to provide hospitality to any who come to their tents. There is a flurry of activity: feet are washed, Sarah cooks bread over hot coals and Abraham fetches a young calf. The text mentions that Abraham 'hurried' to meet them and to get the meal prepared, indicating the importance of hospitality. Under the shade of a nearby tree Abraham's guests are replenished. It is interesting to note that the Gospels frequently picture Jesus at a meal (such as in Matt. 9:9–13, Mark 1:29–31, Luke 7:36–50; 10:38–42 and John 2:1–11).

As the conversation turns to the delicate matter of children, Abraham becomes aware that he is in the presence of the Lord (Adonai in Hebrew) Exalted One and chapter 19 verse 1 reveals the other two, as angels. Sarah is obviously eavesdropping from the tent and is bowled over by the question, 'Where is Sarah?' and by the prophetic utterance about the immanence of conception. The delay of twenty-four years since the original calling was part of God's plan to develop their faith. We are often so eager for God to act that we forget that He wants to develop us as His disciples primarily, and not just supply our whims or desires! For Sarah it was total incongruity: she felt old and was long past the menstrual cycle. No wonder she laughs to herself at this impossibility, for maybe she had resigned herself to the idea that she would never bear children. Sarah needed to learn that the God who brought them from Mesopotamia was a God of surprises. Are we sometimes tempted to limit God by our theological assumptions? Mike Yaconelli once wrote, 'How did we end up so comfortable with God? How did our awe of God get reduced to a lukewarm appreciation of God?"

As the three visitors leave, God pauses to speak to His friend Abraham. Acknowledging afresh His purposes for Abraham and his family, God shares His heart over the sinfulness of Sodom and Gomorrah. The two angels depart to find out the full extent of the wickedness of the two cities. God already knew the facts because of his omniscience, but His judgment is always tempered by mercy. The conversation that ensues is not bargaining or persuasion, for Abraham already knows that wrongdoing has to be punished. His question is about the innocent minority and whether God would stop the judgment for fifty God-honouring people. As the number reduces to ten (vv26–32), Abraham understands that God knows best and will do what is right.

Although Abraham may have been pleading with God for the sake of Lot, the rescue is by no means certain. Chapter 19 paints a sad picture of a society consumed by violence and sexual abuse, where forced intimacy was acceptable. The angels found Lot and having confounded the evil sexual intent of the citizens of Sodom they provided safe passage for the family. Peter, writing many years later concerning righteous Lot (2 Pet. 2:7–10a), suggests that Lot was concerned about Sodom's moral corruption. While the angels enforced the flight from the city, Lot's wife may still have hankered after her former life. There are plenty of unanswered questions here but we may be sure that God desires to show mercy even in the most extreme sinful situations.

*M. Yaconelli, *Dangerous Wonder* (Colorado Springs: Nav Press, 1998) p111.

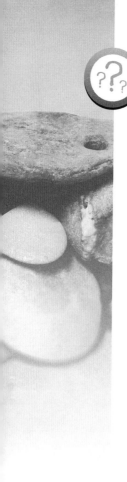

Discussion Starters

1. Read Romans 12:13 and 1 Peter 4:9, where the writers commend the practice of hospitality. How good is your church or group in this department? What are the barriers that we have to overcome in order to grow in the grace of hospitality?

_____

_____

_____

_____

2. Sarah needed to be confronted with the truth about her laughter. Has God ever put His finger on something that you needed to be honest about? If you are able, share something that was a life changer for you.

_____

_____

_____

_____

3. Does the prayer life of Abraham have any relevance for Christians today?

_____

_____

_____

_____

4. Think about your prayer life and how you would like it to improve. What works for you that might be helpful to share with others in the group?

_____

_____

_____

_____

5. The phrase 'Will the Judge of all the earth do right' may be tough to defend in the light of many disasters in our world. Discuss what your response would be to a friend or colleague who challenges you with this issue.

_____

_____

_____

_____

6. Think about the character of Lot as he is depicted in Genesis 12–19 and 2 Peter 2:6–10. What can we learn from him? Did he miss the warning signs when moving to Sodom?

_____

_____

_____

_____

7. Why do you think that Lot's sons-in-law thought he was joking in Genesis 19:14? Does it suggest anything about the way Lot handled his life in Sodom?

_____

_____

_____

_____

8. Many have written over the years about 'the God of surprises'. How has He surprised you recently and caused you to think about His awesome nature and power?

_____

_____

_____

_____

Personal Application

Many people shy away from evangelism because it sometimes conjures up unhelpful memories from the past. What if we followed the examples of Abraham or the many people of the New Testament who opened their homes up to share hospitality? Over a meal people tend to relax and conversation becomes more natural. You don't have to be a great chef; useful ideas are frequently shared on TV or on the internet. People today are aching for meaningful relationships where they are accepted and acknowledged. Maybe you could work together with someone else in your group to plan such a venture. You do not have to preach but just be prayerful for opportunities to share your love for Jesus.

Seeing Jesus in the Scriptures

Abraham learned many lessons as he progressed in his pilgrimage of faith, particularly concerning prayer. Often we find him speaking with God and building altars, where he and others could meet with God. There is growing intimacy as El Shaddai shares with His friend. Jesus also models this relationship of intimacy and fellowship with His Father. The prayer life of Jesus was very varied – sometimes public prayer (Mark 14:35; Luke 3:21), times spent away from people (Luke 6:12; 9:18) and at other times instructing and modelling (Matt. 6:5–15). If Jesus placed so much importance on prayer then we also need to enrol in His school of prayer! *Prayer Coach* by James Nicodem is a helpful resource.

WEEK 5

Test of Faith
(Genesis 21-22)

Opening Icebreaker

Give everyone a piece of paper with the words 'FAITH' and 'TRUST' written at the top. What other words can you think of that have a similar meaning, such as 'confidence'? Write them all down. You may also like to come up with an acrostic for the words – each letter spells out another word connected with 'FAITH' or 'TRUST'.

Bible Readings

- Genesis 21–22
- Job 1
- Matthew 14:22–33
- Matthew 17:14–21
- Mark 2:1–12
- Luke 7:1–10

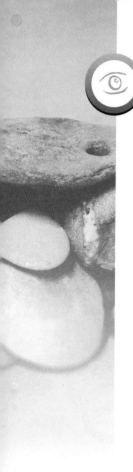

Opening Our Eyes

What rejoicing there must have been in Abraham's camp when Sarah's son, Isaac, was born. The name Isaac means 'He laughs', a parody perhaps on the laughter of Sarah that accompanied the announcement to Abraham in Genesis 18. The months of pregnancy must have seemed endless as they could hardly take it in that they would have a son. God had kept His promises and their faith must have soared. However, the tension between Sarah and her servant Hagar caused much sadness in the camp. On the occasion of Isaac's weaning, he would have been probably about three years old, Ishmael, now a teenager, poked fun at Sarah and Isaac. The reaction of Sarah is to have Hagar thrown out (Gen. 21:10; also look at Gal. 4:21–31). Abraham seems more laid back about the situation due to his fatherly love and responsibilities towards Ishmael, but he hears from God that he should let them leave and that God will take care of them. Sometimes we are faced by tough choices and there may not be an obvious clear path that we can see. It is then that we need to pause and trust God to make it plain.

Hagar exited the camp and wandered in the wilderness. About to give up and prepared for the inevitable, she was surprised by the intervention of 'the angel of the LORD' (Gen. 16:7). This time God speaks from heaven, giving her a further promise for Ishmael's future and water to relieve their immediate thirst. Notice again something of the graciousness of God in the way that He never gave up on Ishmael (Gen. 21:20) and kept His promise (Gen. 17:20).

A well dispute with Abimelech's servants dominates the end of chapter 21. Abraham had previously moved his camp into Philistine territory and now together they conclude a peace treaty (Gen. 21:32). Look back at chapter 20, and explore more of the story of Abimelech, a king amongst the Philistines. Abraham seemed to have forgotten all that he learnt in Egypt many years before and fell into the same trap of naming Sarah as his sister! It caused confusion and illness for Abimelech and his household, which was only righted when Abraham faces his sinful behaviour and prayed for their healing. Now, as they conclude a treaty or parity covenant over the area of Beersheba, it is interesting to note the observation of Abimelech in Genesis 21:22. I wonder whether the people that we live and work with recognise that God is at work in our lives?

Abraham faced his toughest test yet when God commanded that he sacrifice his precious son Isaac on Mount Moriah. He had already surrendered his home and family in leaving Mesopotamia and given up his rights to the fertile pastureland by Jordan. Abraham does not procrastinate or question, demonstrating his obedience by taking along wood for the sacrifice. One can only imagine the tricky conversation with Isaac as they made their way to the top of the hill and prepared the altar. A key verse here is Genesis 22:8, where Abraham asserts his faith in God's provision, even believing in resurrection from the dead (Heb. 11:17–19). Also see his word to his servants in Genesis 22:5, 'we will come back to you'. So Abraham demonstrates the reality of his continuing faith in God and receives again a renewal of God's covenant blessing. He had learned that obedience and faith are crucial in his journey with God.

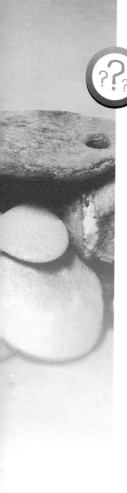

Discussion Starters

1. The Bible regards joy as being an essential characteristic of the Christian life (see John 16:22; 17:13, Gal. 5:22; Phil. 4:4). Discuss how this works out in your daily living.

_____

_____

_____

_____

_____

2. Family arguments are never pleasant. What advice would you have offered to Sarah and Hagar to help them work through their rivalry?

_____

_____

_____

_____

_____

3. Sarah makes reference to Hagar in derogatory terms in Genesis 21:10. Do we use unhelpful words about others who are different to us? How do they reinforce our prejudices?

_____

_____

_____

_____

_____

4. Sometimes tough decisions have to be made for the greater good. Imagine Abraham's sadness at saying farewell to Ishmael. What complicated decisions are you facing right now?

_____

_____

_____

_____

5. In the light of Genesis 20, what stories could you share about the grace of God reaching out to you even when you had messed up your life?

_____

_____

_____

_____

_____

6. Abraham was willing to sacrifice his treasured son in order to be obedient to God. Have there been times in your life when you have had to be willing to surrender to the call of God?

_____

_____

_____

_____

_____

7. What does it mean to fear God? Abraham obviously did in Genesis 22:12, but what does that mean for us today?

_____

_____

_____

_____

_____

8. Make a list of the ways that Abraham serves as both an example and a warning to us.

_____

_____

_____

_____

_____

Personal Application

The story of Abraham is littered with promises and Abraham learnt that through faith, he was an inheritor of the great promises of God for his family. Spend some time thinking back over your journey as a Christian and recall the promises that God has made to you. Give thanks for the ones that have or are being presently fulfilled. There may be some that are still pending! Find a notebook and write them down so that you do not forget them. On a weekly basis pray over those not yet fulfilled and trust God through all your doubts and perplexities that He will do what He has promised. What does God want to teach you during this waiting time?

Seeing Jesus in the Scriptures

In the Gospel narratives we read of Jesus ministering to people who were sick and needing healing. The accounts are very varied but evidence of faith is one similarity that runs through all of them. Sometimes faith is exercised by the person themselves, like with the woman with a blood problem in Luke 8:40–48. At other times it is demonstrated by others, as with the man let down through the roof in Mark 2:1–12. God loves it when we learn to trust Him and take Him at His word. Abraham and Sarah were on a journey with God and their faith would be stretched throughout their lives. Just as God promised to be with Abraham, so too He is with you. As someone has said, 'Faith – it does not make things easy it makes them possible' (see also Luke 1:37).

WEEK 6

Practical Faith
(Genesis 24)

Opening Icebreaker

Have you ever been travelling somewhere and lost your
way? Consider the factors that caused the loss of direction.
Maybe the navigator was at fault or the GPS system was
not programmed correctly, or perhaps you did not listen
to instructions? Consider together what is most important
when you are seeking to know God's will for your life.

Bible Readings

- Genesis 24
- Exodus 15:13
- Psalm 23
- Proverbs 3:5,6; 16:9
- Isaiah 30:21
- Acts 16:6–10

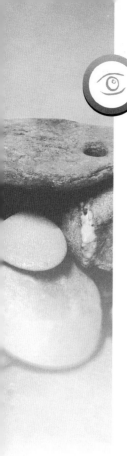

Opening Our Eyes

Chapter 24 opens with Abraham's concern for his unmarried son Isaac, who was nearing his fortieth birthday in Genesis 25:20. Knowing the problems that marrying a local girl might bring for a son of the covenant, Abraham sent his trusted servant, possibly Eliezer, referred to in Genesis 15:2, to his relatives in Harran. Abraham already knew that his brother Nahor had eight sons (Gen. 22:20,23) and it was a fair assumption that one of them would have a daughter of the right age! Abraham maintained that the girl needed to come to Canaan rather than Isaac return to Harran. Like Abraham, when we set a course for following God wherever He leads, there can be no turning back (Luke 9:62).

There is real confidence of faith as Abraham sent his servant on the long journey. He knew that the God who had called him and had provided for him throughout his life was not about to forget him now. On the swearing of a solemn oath, the servant follows Abraham's instructions and takes with him gifts for the family. Notice how the servant combines common sense and dependence upon God's guidance in Genesis 24:11–14. At Nahor he waits by the well, knowing that women would come there to draw water at the end of the day, but also aware that the venture was not going to be accomplished by human wisdom alone. Before finishing his prayer a beautiful young woman named Rebekah appears at the well to fetch water for her family, and the test he had engineered with God falls into place as she offered to water his camels. The ensuing conversation confirmed for the elderly servant that God is in this meeting and he bowed to worship God. He referred to God as being the God of Abraham but his prayer conversation indicated that he too had a relationship with God. Notice in his prayer the servant claimed that he was quite unworthy of this work of God – 'As for me', even me – which demonstrates that this situation has blown him away. When did you last worship with a real sense of awe of God and your own unworthiness?

As the servant is taken to the home of Bethuel, another nephew of Abraham and father of Rebekah and Laban, he quickly outlines why he had come the 400 miles or so from Canaan. The test he had devised was important because it showed the servant something of Rebekah's inner character and her ability to manage a regular household task. Actually giving water to ten thirsty camels was no mean feat, as they are capable of drinking 25 gallons of water after a long journey! Family negotiations ensue, which involved gifts being given and promises being exchanged. Everyone agreed that this was a remarkable work of God to bring the servant to Nahor. The only point to be discussed further was the timing of Rebekah's journey to Canaan, and her agreement meant that the journey could start almost immediately.

The first meeting between Isaac and Rebekah is like a classic movie scene. Although Isaac is unable to see Rebekah's face before their wedding, he is immediately drawn to her in love. They would face many challenges in the future and their family life would be pressurised by conflicting loyalties, but for now they could bask in the delight of their new-found love.

Discussion Starters

1. What are the chief concerns expressed by Abraham in Genesis 24:1–9? Why were they so important?

   Not to take a wife from Canaanite

2. How do you think the trusted servant felt as he journeyed towards Nahor?

   Worried

3. What practical advice, encouragement and help can your church offer to those who are struggling with singleness?

4. Spend some time sharing with the group about how God has guided you over recent years. Finding God's way is never easy but what are the most important principles you have learnt?

   Prayer is good

5. Do you think it is ever right to ask God for a sign when we are seeking His will? Check out Judges 6:36–40. What are the possible dangers of this approach?

6. The servant appears to test Rebekah to see whether she is a suitable partner for Isaac. What do you think he discovered? See Genesis 24:15–25.

7. Why do you think that Laban was so eager to hurry to the well and meet Abraham's servant in Genesis 24:28–31? You will find further information in the later story of Jacob in Genesis 29–30.

8. We often speak of God's providential care for His people. What indications do you find of this in chapter 24, and what can you learn from it?

Practical Application

Finding God's will for our lives is often fraught with difficulty and uncertainty. There is no magical formula in the Bible. Prayer, the advice of others and circumstances all play their part in confirming the direction God wants us to go. He wants us to follow Him and walk in ways pleasing to Him as part of our daily devotion. So it is a continual, moment-by-moment obedience that we should exercise. We should do the next thing at hand and trust Him to redirect if necessary. Look at the way Paul and his team worked: they simply moved from town to town sharing the good news, but only at Troas do they pause to await further instructions, when the Holy Spirit stopped them in their tracks (Acts 16). As Isaiah 30:21 suggests, it is when we turn off God's pathway that we hear His voice saying, 'This is the way; walk in it'.

Seeing Jesus in the Scriptures

The amazing work completed by Abraham's servant in bringing Isaac's bride from Nahor to Canaan may give us a fleeting insight into the work of the Holy Spirit, who is God's agent in bringing people to Christ. Look again at the unfolding story in Genesis 24 and see the parallels with your own story of faith development. God took the initiative, looked for us when we were far away from Him and brought us to Him. Now loved as His beautiful bride – the Church – we can confidently affirm that we are part of His beloved family. What an incredible story of grace, hope and faith.

WEEK 7

Fellowship of Faith
(Genesis 23; 25:1-11)

Opening Icebreaker

You have been marooned on a desert island and apart from food and supplies the only thing left in your possession is a picture of someone special. It could be a family member, friend or a person in history. Share with the group who that person is and why they mean so much to you. You may like to have a brief prayer time giving thanks for those you have remembered.

Bible Readings

- Genesis 23; 25:1–11
- Numbers 13:22
- Joshua 14:6–15; 15:13–19
- 2 Samuel 2:3–4a
- Hebrews 12:1–3

Opening Our Eyes

Whilst camped near Kiriath Arba, or Hebron, Abraham had to face up to the cruel reality of the death of his precious wife Sarah. They had been companions for seventy or eighty years and had experienced together the bittersweet times that accompanied their earthly pilgrimage. As Abraham bowed by his loved one and wept, perhaps we can feel a little of his grief and pain. We do not read of Abraham weeping apart from this passage, although maybe as he interceded for the safety of his nephew Lot there were tears. Family bereavements are always times when we think back and trawl through our memories. Abraham could reflect on the excitement of their faith journey but also the shame of long-term childlessness and the disappointments of failure and deception. If you know someone who is facing loss and the sadness of bereavement perhaps you could think of ways that you could encourage and support them.

The resulting conversation with the Hittite leaders regarding a burial place for Sarah is interesting as it follows widespread customs common at the time in the Hittite Empire. It took place at the gate of the city (Gen. 23:18), the place where civic and judicial matters were settled. As a man of honour Abraham refused the free gift of the field that included the cave of Machpelah and some trees. The 400 shekel price agreed was probably high but Abraham was in no mood to haggle. It is an interesting point highlighted by some commentators that although he held the title deeds of the land given to him by God, this is his first actual purchase of a piece of land! For more, see Genesis 13:14–17 and Acts 7:5; as Abraham says, 'I am a foreigner and stranger among you' (Gen. 23:4). The writer to the Hebrews picks up this thought in 11:13–14, declaring that the heavenly vision of a celestial city is a far better option! Where are our sights set? Are we looking forward to being with Christ? If so, let us not get too comfortable here!

It seems that Abraham lived for another thirty-five years after the death of Sarah and would have probably seen his grandsons, Esau and Jacob, grow into their teenage years. Interestingly, Ishmael returned to help Isaac bury their father, alongside Sarah in the cave of Machpelah. Kiriath Arba is sometimes given an alternative name – Hebron – such as in Genesis 23:2,19; this is translated to mean fellowship or communion. It was a very special place for Abraham's descendents as it was the place where Abraham settled after separating from Lot and where he built an altar. At this place Abraham met with God and in the intimacy of the moment, received the promise of the land. It was where three visitors came to tell Abraham and Sarah that the childless years were over and where Abraham again spoke boldly with God. No wonder that when the twelve spies visited the land, as described in Numbers 13–14, that Caleb was determined to stake his claim to the promised land in that place. Read Joshua 14:6–15 and observe how Caleb had carried the dream of a home in Hebron for forty-five years, believing the promise of Moses (Josh. 14:9). Hebron was a rugged mountain inhabited by the strongest and most powerful of the Anakite people, yet Caleb viewed it as a place of blessing and was determined whatever the cost to make it his home. It was here that David was first anointed king over Judah and later all Israel (2 Sam. 2:1–4; 5:1–5).

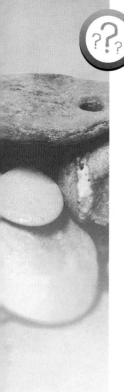

Discussion Starters

1. C.S. Lewis said, 'No one ever told me that grief felt so like fear.'* How can we help people who are struggling in this area? Are there any practical steps we can take to support those who are anxious and fearful?

[handwritten] Hospitality   Spend time with people?

2. Why did Abraham think it was so important to buy the cave of Machpelah?

[handwritten] How could anyone accuse God's promise to take advantage because of God's provision

3. Can we learn anything from the way that Abraham negotiated with the Hittite leaders?

[handwritten] He was honest   He did not take advantage

4. Look again at the story of Caleb in Numbers 13–14 and Joshua 13, and discuss the fearsome determination that drove him through the forty years of wilderness wandering. What lessons can we learn from it?

5. Joshua 15 suggests that Caleb was not the only one blessed by the conquest of Hebron. How can we turn our blessings into positive encouragements for others?

Show how God provided

6. Abraham, in his limited understanding, was looking for something beyond his earthly life in Hebrews 11:10. What about us? How can we be less entangled with the clutter of things? (See Phil. 3:17–21.)

By keeping everything under control

7. What lessons have you learnt from the story of Abraham?

Trust + obey. Follow + follow God's instructions

8. Try to sum up Abraham's life in one sentence.

Trusting + following God

---

*C.S. Lewis, *A Grief Observed* (London: Faber & Faber, 1966).

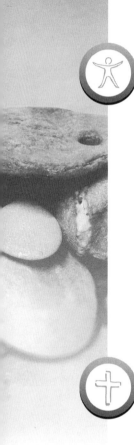

Personal Application

We can become very comfortable in our Christian lives and that can lead to introversion where we protect ourselves from the pain of the world around. It is interesting to note that Abraham showed concern and practical action when others were hurting (see Gen. 14:1–17; 18:16–33). What issue is God stirring you up about in your world? It could be the horror of human slavery, poverty in your community or maybe the care of elderly people. First of all pray about it and search for information. Look for others with similar concerns and see if you can possibly partner with them. Check out the story of Blake Mycoskie, who found a way to practically help poor people in South America, Ethiopia, Rwanda and South Africa (see en.wikipedia.org/wiki/Toms_Shoes). Find a project that you can work with and volunteer.

Seeing Jesus in the Scriptures

I love the resurrection story of the two disciples on their way to Emmaus. When they were least expecting it Jesus found them and walked with them. It seems that all their hopes had been dashed and the future was dark. Yet as they talked along the way they began to understand that God had greater purposes than what they had ever dreamed about. Abraham discovered that wherever he went, God was present, even when he had spoilt things by being devious and going his own way, and in the heartbreaking times too. Saint Augustine is reputed to have once said, 'Trust the past to the mercy of God, the present to His Love and the future to His Providence.'

Leader's Notes

Week 1: Faith and Disobedience

Opening Icebreaker

Abraham seems to have been afraid of the implications of moving his family to Egypt. So in this icebreaker make opportunities for group members to share about fearful situations they have been through in the past and tease out what strategies can be put into place to help in the future. This may need careful handling with some who are very anxious.

Aim of the Session

To recognise the importance of God's call on our lives and the costs of being obedient.

Discussion Starters

1. This open question gives opportunity for people to share the things that particularly stood out for them in the passage. This could be a starter for each session to encourage people to open up and start talking.

2. You might like to choose a couple of group members to role play this conversation between Abraham and Sarah, without a set script! You will need to be sure that they are comfortable with this and are able to carry it off! It should lead to some helpful discussion about marriage!

3. Initially, focus your discussion around the idea of stepping out into a darkened room. Some might be willing to share about times in their lives when they felt

called by God to do a similar thing. You might also look at the way the disciples in Luke 5 left their nets and followed Jesus. Are there any other biblical examples?

4. Think through the possible reasons why Lot left Harran with Abraham – a favourite nephew perhaps, or did Lot catch the vision behind the move? This should lead you into a discussion about obedience to God and what it really looks like today.

5. At this point a piece of paper and a pen might help people to write down the marker points in their lives. Draw a straight line to illustrate your discipleship journey and put circles around the important times like coming to faith, hearing God's call, discovering your spiritual gift or moving home. Group members might like to share with the group one such significant time.

6. Here you might return to the issue of fear and the reasons behind Abraham's behaviour in Egypt. Certainly he wobbled at this point in his faith but did he learn any lessons about himself and about God? How is God's grace shown in this passage?

7. This might require you as leader to give an example to get things going. Do concentrate on the ways that God was able to get you back on track. You could just quickly review the story of the prophet Jonah and the way that God graciously dealt with him. This quote might be helpful from Edwin Cole, 'Obedience is an act of faith; disobedience is the result of unbelief.'*

8. There are many examples in the Bible where God restored someone who had messed up their life. Think about Peter at the trial of Jesus, denying Him three times, or John Mark, who left Paul's first mission journey to return home. Discuss the whole idea of mercy and grace as expressions of God's character and how they balance with His justice. Have you experienced this in your life?

*Edwin Cole, www.edcole.org Under the 'Coleisms' tab, search for 'Obedience'.

Week 2: The Generosity of Faith

Opening Icebreaker

Often there are people in our communities who are struggling and will not seek help from the official channels, perhaps because of pride. As a group you might identify who they are and think of ways that you could assist without compromising their self-worth. It might be that some random act of kindness could open the way for a deeper conversation about Jesus.

Aim of the Session

To remind ourselves afresh of God's bountiful grace and understand how we who have received grace can demonstrate that same grace to others.

Discussion Starters

1. How many of us have a desire to be more financially secure, even though compared to the rest of the world we are wealthy? How do we handle our present finances and are we honouring God with what we have? Paul talked about being content with his situation (Phil. 4:12) and was confident in God's generous provision (4:19). Share how we can develop a generosity of spirit.

2. Again this is a tough question but worth exploring in the safety of the group. Take the lead and share something of your journey. Make sure that you point

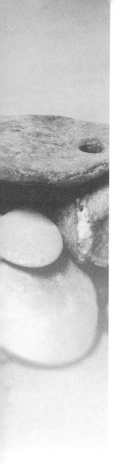

out what you have learnt through the experience and your honesty should help others to share also.

3. Think through the amazing promises God gives to Abraham in Genesis 13:14–17. Abraham may have given away the fertile land near the Jordan River but God gives him the assurance that all the land of Canaan is his. After generously blessing Lot, Abraham discovers that you cannot out-give God. Why is this important for Abraham to understand?

4. The subject of conflict in the Church is very troubling. Do not allow this to degenerate into a session of moans and grumbles about your church. If there are issues that are particularly relevant for some in the group, tease them out gently and seek to give positives from the other side. An old boss of mine used to say 'OFM' – there is always one fact more! Do pray about these things and perhaps for other places where conflict is rampant.

5. Here you might do some research on the internet about the horrors of twenty-first century slavery and some organisations are suggested. Sometimes people struggle to see what they can do to make things any different. Perhaps you could arrange an event at your church to highlight the needs or devote one Sunday service to the topic. Maybe some excerpts from the DVD *Amazing Grace* might help here. Matt Redman has a song written for the A21 Campaign called *Let my people go*.

6. Review the passage from Hebrews 7 regarding Melchizedek and consider whether he was a foreshadowing of Christ. The story follows the defeat of the five kings and rescue of Lot, so centres on the theme of thanksgiving. Help the group to find ways of expressing their thanks for the blessings they have received. Note what Paul says in Colossians 2:6–7.

7. The way that we give is often an indication of how thankful we are. Share ideas of how we can make giving more part of the way that we live. People might like to share their experiences of giving and the blessings they have received. Tithing may just be a good starting point for Christian giving, so help the group to relax and not be caught up by regulations.

8. It is an interesting question as to why Abraham refused to keep the spoils from his raid. Was it just that he did not want to be beholden to the King of Sodom or was there another reason? Is there a principle for us to consider here? Would we accept a lottery win?

Week 3: Faith for the Future

Opening Icebreaker

Encourage the group to be honest in this exercise and take the time to think about their own personal fears. Make sure there is privacy and that the cards or paper slips are filled in anonymously. Note what are the common fears of the group, making sure people respect one another so that unique concerns are not trivialised. Suggestions should be shared about ways to combat fear, and then pray for each other.

Aim of the Session

To understand how Abraham trusted that God would keep His promises and how that trust in the faithfulness of God was the basis of his acceptance.

Discussion Starters

1. Most of the group will probably be able to share about times in their lives when they were

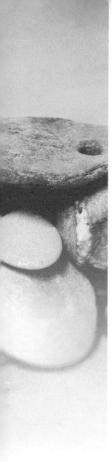

going through tough times and heard God speak assurance about His closeness. This could be when reading the Bible, through a prophetic word or perhaps in a church service. Be prepared for some quirky stories but do not dismiss them! The last sentence of Matthew 28 may help.

2. Some in your group may well be able to identify with Abraham's fear of childlessness, so handle carefully! However, there is a good conversation to be engaged in concerning how you can help people struggling in this area. How can we avoid the mistake of not allowing God to keep His promises in His way?

3. The doctrine of justification by faith is not easy to understand. Review the Romans 4 passage and compare it with Genesis 15:6. Remember that this took place before the Law was given in the time of Moses. So the basis of acceptance by God was by grace through faith in His promise. Discuss the folly of depending on human action alone.

4. Try to imagine if God asked you the same questions that He asked Hagar in Genesis 16:8. What would be your answer? Spend some time thinking through the issues here of personal identity. Look up the words of Paul recorded in Acts 27:23 and discuss his confidence in God.

5. There may be people in your group who feel disappointed with God because a dream was not realised or a promise they felt God had made to them is as yet unfulfilled. Discuss how we wait for God and how we can learn to trust Him better. Philip Yancey's book *Disappointment with God* might be helpful.

6. Discuss how we should respond to the great ethical problems of our day, like surrogacy, assisted death and biogenetics.

7. Share experiences when the presence of God was very tangible. Be aware that there may be some in the group who have never experienced this and feel they are missing out, so be sensitive how you share and encourage people to be open to what God may want to do in their lives. Take some time to listen to God and pray for each other.

8. Ask the group about their ongoing relationship with God. Do they feel that they are growing in that relationship and their intimacy with God? Explore how free they feel to be able to be themselves and to even laugh in God's presence. How does your church or group encourage that relationship to go deeper?

Week 4: The Prayer of Faith

Opening Icebreaker

If you use a concordance and do an internet search you should find some excellent quotes about prayer. Each person should have at least one quote printed out for them. Share together the things you can learn about prayer from the quotes. Maybe you could have a poll to see which one you feel to be the most helpful.

Aim of the Session

To remind us that prayer is a conversation with God and to discover, as Abraham did, that as God's friends we can debate and plead with Him. Prayer does certainly change things, especially the person who prays.

Discussion Starters

1. It is always good to be invited out for a meal. The practice of hospitality seems to be encouraged

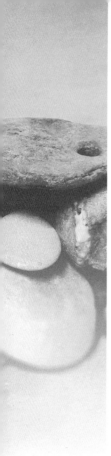

in the New Testament and the passages from Romans 12:13 and 1 Peter 4:9 should be read together. Do you have common meals together as a group? How much is this encouraged in your church? How can we overcome any barriers in making this work?

2. Discuss in the group how easy it is to bring a challenge to a friend who is in danger of compromising their faith. Has anyone ever needed to challenge you? How easy is it to honestly face up to such a challenge?

3. Examine the prayer life of Abraham. Revisit those sections that are relevant, like Genesis 15:2–9; 17; 18:16–33. Should we follow these examples and are there principles that are relevant for us today?

4. Share with each other things that help you to have an effective prayer life. Do you have a pattern for prayer like the acrostic CHAT: Confess, Honour, Ask and Thank? Are there areas that you would like to improve? As has been said, 'Fail to plan, plan to fail.'

5. Talking about our response to disaster may well prove helpful to some in the group who struggle themselves or have friends that do. You can read endless books on apologetics and search the internet for help, but the main thing is that we listen to the concerns of others. Our answers must never be arrogant or trite and we may need to own up that we just do not know. Always remember that God is sovereign (see Gen. 18:25 and Job 42:1–3).

6. Spend some time looking up other Bible passages about Lot, such as 2 Peter 2:6–10, Luke 17:28–9,32, as well as Genesis 12–19. What was Lot like in terms of his character? How aware do you think he was of the evil around him in Sodom? Had insipidness crept into his heart so that even the incest of 19:30–38 was not challenged? He could have returned to Abraham and found new sons-in-law there.

7. This connects with the previous question but it is an interesting question as to why his sons-in-law thought the impending judgment was a joke! Was his warning completely out of character from how he normally lived? You might like to explore issues about the way we live amongst our friends. How can we maintain a radical difference without being weird and odd?

8. Allow people in the group to share about times when God has surprised them. Some may want to talk about times long ago and that may be where you need to start, but try to encourage up-to-date stories to be shared. Think too of Bible figures that God surprised, such as Zechariah and Mary, both in Luke 1.

Week 5: Test of Faith

Opening Icebreaker

Prepare your pieces of paper with two words, 'FAITH' and 'TRUST', written at the top. This exercise can be done in pairs or as individuals. You might have a large sheet of paper or a white board to collect all the suggestions. Make sure everyone's contribution is valued! Working out an acrostic on the word 'FAITH' can be done together. If you struggle with the acrostic you may cheat by consulting the internet!

Aim of the Session

To examine faith under pressure and learn from the example of Abraham. How did he cope with God's

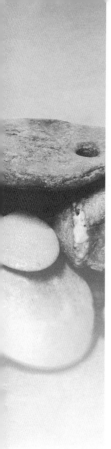

command to sacrifice Isaac and facing the possibility of losing his and Sarah's precious son? What lessons can we learn to help us when our faith is stretched?

Discussion Starters

1. As you read through the suggested passages, think about how important joy is to a Christian.

2. Perhaps you could ask two of your group to perform an impromptu role play of Sarah and Hagar discussing the relative merits of their children. Think through the common issues that cause family arguments for us today. Are there insights that will help us deal with the issues and not bury them to be brought out later?

3. In her anger Sarah was harsh with Hagar, perhaps forgetting that it was her idea in the first place to go down the surrogacy route! Think about the ways that we are unhelpful in the things that we say, especially about those who are not like us. Do we have prejudices towards others even in the Church? The TV comedy *Keeping up Appearances* has some good examples of this!

4. It would be good to share about times in your lives when difficult decisions have had to be made for the common good. Try to enter into Abraham's anguish as he said farewell to Ishmael. Although not the inheritor of the promise made to Abraham, Ishmael was important to him. It would be good to pray for one another if there are some difficult decisions to be made.

5. In Genesis 20 we find that Abraham has again fallen into the trap of deception. Why do you think that Abraham still had not learnt his lesson? What other Bible stories illustrate the grace of God at work, even when people messed up their lives? What stories does the group have to share in this area?

6. Perhaps there have been times in the personal lives of the group members when they experienced God's call to surrender something they held dear, such as leaving a well-paid job in order to serve God elsewhere. Think about the cost involved and how God honours that obedience.

7. This is another tricky question because fearing God is very different from the way that we use the word 'fear' in ordinary life. It is clear if you look at the story of Joseph, great grandson of Abraham, in Genesis 39 and 42:18 that fearing God is positive for it saves Joseph from giving in to his sinful nature. A God-fearing person is to be trusted because they are more likely to keep their word. Tease out other ideas that resonate in our time.

8. This is another pencil and paper exercise for the group. Make two columns and head them 'example' and 'warning'. Encourage everyone to contribute and pray about the challenges that emerge.

Week 6: Practical Faith

Opening Icebreaker

Draw out stories of times when people discovered that they were lost. Do not allow this to deteriorate into a male/female discussion about who is best at navigating! Stereotypes are not helpful here. What were people feeling – anger, frustration, fear or anything else? Think about what steps had to be taken in order to return to the right track, such as stopping and asking the way!

Aim of the Session

To understand something more of the way that God guides us.

Discussion Starters

1. Finding a bride for Isaac was important to Abraham in order to continue the family line, and his role was an expected one of a father at that time in Middle Eastern history. This time Abraham was not overstepping the mark! Think about his concerns if Isaac found a Canaanite wife. Tease out why these were important to the family.

2. Spend some time imagining what would have been going through the mind of the servant as he travelled towards the north. Perhaps pleasure at being chosen for the task, tempered by concerns about the possible outcomes. The indications are that he was mindful that this had to be a God-directed operation.

3. In an age when people marry much later in life, we may not fully understand Abraham's concern for Isaac. Churches have in the past seemed to have been more anxious about married people than singles. How can we readdress this issue and be more encouraging towards those struggling with singleness?

4. As leader of the group share your own personal experience of God's guidance. What are the important principles that should guide our walk with God? It might be helpful to list these for future reference. Try to bring out the fact that God wants us to travel with Him, constantly led by His Spirit and open to the promptings of His voice. There may be many ways that God speaks to us such as through the Bible, other people or a prophetic word.

5. Thinking about the story of Gideon in Judges 6:36 and this one in Genesis 24, there was the use of a sign. Do you think that asking God for a sign is appropriate? There is a lovely scene in *Bruce Almighty* where the main character asks God for a sign but cannot see it when it happens! Can you think of possible dangers with this approach?

6. Read again the story of the meeting of the servant with Rebekah at the well. What were the tests that he set her? Did he discover any significant flaws or attributes? What about her character – are there any indications in the passage of what she was like as a person?

7. Spend some time considering Rebekah's brother Laban. As you play detective, are there any significant character flaws in this man? Look at verse 30. Check the story of Jacob and his father-in-law in Genesis 29–31. What can we learn from Laban's behaviour?

8. What evidence can you find in this chapter about the providential care of God? J. Vernon McGee says, 'Providence is the means by which God directs all things – both animate and inanimate, seen and unseen, good and evil – toward a worthy purpose, which means His will must finally prevail.'* Read Romans 8:28 also.

* J. Vernon McGee, *Thru the Bible Vol. 15: History of Israel (Ezra/Nehemiah/Esther)* (Thomas Nelson: 1997).

Week 7: Fellowship of Faith

Opening Icebreaker

It might be a good idea to warn the group about this icebreaker the week before. This gives them time to think about the person they will be sharing about and prepare a few thoughts. Perhaps people could bring a photograph of that person to the group that might make the session more real. Be aware that some people will want to share

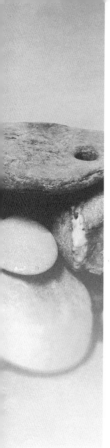

but will find it difficult. When you have finished sharing, spend some time in prayer giving thanks for the ones that have been mentioned.

Aim of the Session

To understand something of the significance of Hebron in the history of God's people.

Discussion Starters

1. Consider the quote from C.S. Lewis. What are the similarities between grief and fear? It maybe that someone in the group would like to share their experience of grief, but do not force this. What sort of things help when someone is going through the pain of loss? Do be practical here and think about ways that those grieving can be supported by your group or church.

2. Abraham was certain that he wanted to buy the cave of Machpelah. Can you think why he was so determined? Did he want to do something special for Sarah and purchase some land where she had lived, in order to keep memories alive? What are some appropriate ways that we can remember those who have passed away?

3. In a culture very familiar with bargaining to decide a deal, it seems that Abraham was quite compliant and Ephron seemed to benefit most from the arrangement. Are we sometimes less than honourable in our eagerness to secure a bargain? The purchase of the field and cave was significant for future generations as Abraham established a tomb for posterity.

4. Caleb is a great character with an insatiable desire to obey and please God (Num. 14:24). Help the group to consider how he felt when God's people had to turn

back to wander forty more years in the wilderness, and yet he had the dream of Hebron ever in his mind. Are there dreams that group members have which are as yet unrealised?

5. Often it is said that we are blessed in order to be a blessing! How have you found that to work out in your life? What opportunities do you have to be a blessing in your area? Share some encouragement with the group.

6. It is easy to be so consumed with life issues in the here and now that we do not think about the reality of life with God in the future. Encourage your group to share about the hopes they have as they contemplate the future. The writer of Hebrews maintains that Abraham only had a hazy view of the future, but he was 'looking forward' (Heb. 11:8–10). Can you think of ways to unclutter your lives?

7. Look back over the studies of the past weeks and list the important lessons you have learnt from the life of Abraham. What difference will they make to your everyday living?

8. Have an idea generating session to summarise the life of Abraham in a sentence! You could perhaps work out an acrostic on the life of Abraham if you want extra material! Steven Kiele wrote this one, 'A man of character, Brilliant in his own way, Rough on the edges, A heart of gold, He was an example, A man worth following, Many of us he inspired.' Check out the website www.joglab.com for help.

Continue transforming your daily walk with God.

Every Day with Jesus

With around half a million readers, this insightful devotional by Selwyn Hughes is one of the most popular daily Bible reading tools in the world. A large-print edition is also available.
72-page booklets, 120x170mm

Life Every Day

Apply the Bible to life each day with these challenging life-application notes written by international speaker and well-known author Jeff Lucas.
64-page booklets, 120x170mm

Inspiring Women Every Day

Written by women for women of all ages and from all walks of life. These notes will help to build faith and bring encouragement and inspiration to the lives and hearts of Christian women.
64-page booklets, 120x170mm

Cover to Cover Every Day

Study one Old Testament and one New Testament book in depth with each issue, and a psalm every weekend. Covers every book of the Bible in five years.
64-page booklets, 120x170mm

For current prices or to order visit www.cwr.org.uk/store
Available online or from Christian bookshops.

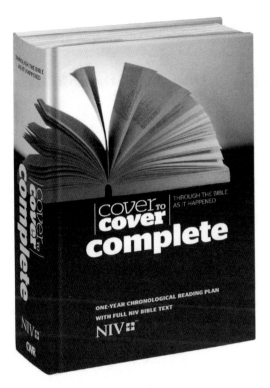

Journey through the Bible as it happened in a year of daily readings

Read through the entire Bible in a year with 366 daily readings from the New International Version (NIV) arranged in chronological order.

Beautiful charts, maps, illustrations and diagrams make the biblical background vivid, timelines enable you to track your progress, and a daily commentary helps you to apply what you read to your life.

A special website also provides character studies, insightful articles, photos of archaeological sites and much more for increased understanding and insight.

Cover to Cover Complete - NIV Edition
1,600 pages, hardback with ribbon marker, 140x215mm
ISBN: 978-1-85345-804-0

Latest resource

Luke – A Prescription for Living
by John Houghton

How should we live in today's world? Luke records in his Gospel a detailed historical account of Jesus and shows us how Jesus provides a prescription for living in today's world, and for the future.

72-page booklet, 210x148mm
ISBN: 978-1-78259-270-9

The bestselling *Cover to Cover* Bible Study Series

1 Corinthians
Growing a Spirit-filled church
ISBN: 978-1-85345-374-8

2 Corinthians
Restoring harmony
ISBN: 978-1-85345-551-3

1 Peter
Good reasons for hope
ISBN: 978-1-78259-088-0

1 Timothy
Healthy churches –
effective Christians
ISBN: 978-1-85345-291-8

23rd Psalm
The Lord is my shepherd
ISBN: 978-1-85345-449-3

2 Timothy and Titus
Vital Christianity
ISBN: 978-1-85345-338-0

Abraham
Adventures of faith
ISBN: 978-1-78259-089-7

Acts 1–12
Church on the move
ISBN: 978-1-85345-574-2

Acts 13–28
To the ends of the earth
ISBN: 978-1-85345-592-6

Barnabas
Son of encouragement
ISBN: 978-1-85345-911-5

Bible Genres
Hearing what the Bible really says
ISBN: 978-1-85345-987-0

Daniel
Living boldly for God
ISBN: 978-1-85345-986-3

Ecclesiastes
Hard questions and
spiritual answers
ISBN: 978-1-85345-371-7

Elijah
A man and his God
ISBN: 978-1-85345-575-9

Ephesians
Claiming your inheritance
ISBN: 978-1-85345-229-1

Esther
For such a time as this
ISBN: 978-1-85345-511-7

Fruit of the Spirit
Growing more like Jesus
ISBN: 978-1-85345-375-5

Galatians
Freedom in Christ
ISBN: 978-1-85345-648-0

Genesis 1–11
Foundations of reality
ISBN: 978-1-85345-404-2

God's Rescue Plan
Finding God's fingerprints
on human history
ISBN: 978-1-85345-294-9

Great Prayers of the Bible
Applying them to our lives today
ISBN: 978-1-85345-253-6

Hebrews
Jesus – simply the best
ISBN: 978-1-85345-337-3

Hosea
The love that never fails
ISBN: 978-1-85345-290-1

Isaiah 1–39
Prophet to the nations
ISBN: 978-1-85345-510-0

Isaiah 40-66
Prophet of restoration
ISBN: 978-1-85345-550-6

James
Faith in action
ISBN: 978-1-85345-293-2

Jeremiah
The passionate prophet
ISBN: 978-1-85345-372-4

John's Gospel
Exploring the seven miraculous signs
ISBN: 978-1-85345-295-6

Joseph
The power of forgiveness and reconciliation
ISBN: 978-1-85345-252-9

Judges 1-8
The spiral of faith
ISBN: 978-1-85345-681-7

Judges 9-21
Learning to live God's way
ISBN: 978-1-85345-910-8

Luke
A prescription for living
ISBN: 978-1-78259-270-9

Mark
Life as it is meant to be lived
ISBN: 978-1-85345-233-8

Moses
Face to face with God
ISBN: 978-1-85345-336-6

Names of God
Exploring the depths of God's character
ISBN: 978-1-85345-680-0

Nehemiah
Principles for life
ISBN: 978-1-85345-335-9

Parables
Communicating God on earth
ISBN: 978-1-85345-340-3

Philemon
From slavery to freedom
ISBN: 978-1-85345-453-0

Philippians
Living for the sake of the gospel
ISBN: 978-1-85345-421-9

Prayers of Jesus
Hearing His heartbeat
ISBN: 978-1-85345-647-3

Proverbs
Living a life of wisdom
ISBN: 978-1-85345-373-1

Revelation 1-3
Christ's call to the Church
ISBN: 978-1-85345-461-5

Revelation 4-22
The Lamb wins! Christ's final victory
ISBN: 978-1-85345-411-0

Rivers of Justice
Responding to God's call to righteousness today
ISBN: 978-1-85345-339-7

Ruth
Loving kindness in action
ISBN: 978-1-85345-231-4

The Covenants
God's promises and their relevance today
ISBN: 978-1-85345-255-0

The Creed
Belief in action
ISBN: 978-1-78259-202-0

The Divine Blueprint
God's extraordinary power in ordinary lives
ISBN: 978-1-85345-292-5

The Holy Spirit
Understanding and experiencing Him
ISBN: 978-1-85345-254-3

The Image of God
His attributes and character
ISBN: 978-1-85345-228-4

The Kingdom
Studies from Matthew's Gospel
ISBN: 978-1-85345-251-2

The Letter to the Colossians
In Christ alone
ISBN: 978-1-85345-405-9

The Letter to the Romans
Good news for everyone
ISBN: 978-1-85345-250-5

The Lord's Prayer
Praying Jesus' way
ISBN: 978-1-85345-460-8

The Prodigal Son
Amazing grace
ISBN: 978-1-85345-412-7

The Second Coming
Living in the light of Jesus' return
ISBN: 978-1-85345-422-6

The Sermon on the Mount
Life within the new covenant
ISBN: 978-1-85345-370-0

The Tabernacle
Entering into God's presence
ISBN: 978-1-85345-230-7

The Ten Commandments
Living God's Way
ISBN: 978-1-85345-593-3

The Uniqueness of our Faith
What makes Christianity distinctive?
ISBN: 978-1-85345-232-1

smallGroup central

All of our small group ideas and resources in one place

Online:

www.smallgroupcentral.org.uk
is an exciting new website filled with
free video teaching, free tools and a
whole host of ideas.

On the road:

We provide a range of seminars
themed for small groups. If you
would like us to bring a seminar to
your local community, contact us at
hello@smallgroupcentral.org.uk

In print:

We publish books, study guides and
DVDs covering an extensive list of
themes, Bible books and life issues.

Log on and find out more at:
www.smallgroupcentral.org.uk

Seminars and events

Waverley Abbey College

Publishing and media

Conference facilities

Transforming lives

CWR's vision is to enable people to experience personal transformation through applying God's Word to their lives and relationships.
Our Bible-based training and resources help people around the world to:
• Grow in their walk with God
• Understand and apply Scripture to their lives
• Resource themselves and their church
• Develop pastoral care and counselling skills
• Train for leadership
• Strengthen relationships, marriage and family life and much more.
Our insightful writers provide daily Bible reading notes and other resources for all ages, and our experienced course designers and presenters have gained an international reputation for excellence and effectiveness.
CWR's Training and Conference Centres in Surrey and East Sussex, England, provide excellent facilities in idyllic settings – ideal for both learning and spiritual refreshment.

CWR
Applying God's Word
to everyday life and relationships

CWR, Waverley Abbey House,
Waverley Lane, Farnham,
Surrey GU9 8EP, UK

Telephone: **+44 (0)1252 784700**
Email: **info@cwr.org.uk**
Website: **www.cwr.org.uk**

Registered Charity No. 294387
Company Registration No. 1990308

NATIONAL DISTRIBUTORS

UK: (and countries not listed below)
CWR, Waverley Abbey House, Waverley Lane, Farnham, Surrey GU9 8EP.
Tel: (01252) 784700 Outside UK (44) 1252 784700 Email: mail@cwr.org.uk

AUSTRALIA: KI Entertainment, Unit 21 317-321 Woodpark Road, Smithfield, New South Wales 2164 Tel: 1 800 850 777 Fax: 02 9604 3699 Email: sales@kientertainment.com.au

CANADA: David C Cook Distribution Canada, PO Box 98, 55 Woodslee Avenue, Paris, Ontario N3L 3E5 Tel: 1800 263 2664 Email: joy.kearley@davidccook.ca

GHANA: Challenge Enterprises of Ghana, PO Box 5723, Accra Tel: (021) 222437/223249 Fax: (021) 226227 Email: ceg@africaonline.com.gh

HONG KONG: Cross Communications Ltd, 11/F Ko's House, 577 Nathan Road, Kowloon Tel: 2780 1188 Fax: 2770 6229 Email: cross@crosshk.com

INDIA: Crystal Communications, Plot No. 125, Road No. 7, T.M.C, Mahendra Hills, East Marredpally, Secunderabad - 500026 Tel/Fax: (040) 27737145 Email: crystal_edwj@rediffmail.com

KENYA: Keswick Books and Gifts Ltd, PO Box 10242-00400, Nairobi Tel: (020) 2226047/312639 Email: sales.keswick@africaonline.co.ke

MALAYSIA: Canaanland Distributors Sdn Bhd, No. 25 Jalan PJU 1A/41B, NZX Commercial Centre, Ara Jaya, 47301 Petaling Jaya, Selangor Tel: (03) 7885 0540/1/2 Fax: (03) 7885 0545 Email: info@canaanland.com.my

Salvation Publishing & Distribution Sdn Bhd, 23 Jalan SS 2/64, 47300 Petaling Jaya, Selangor Tel: (03) 78766411/78766797 Fax: (03) 78757066/78756360 Email: info@ salvationbookcentre.com

NEW ZEALAND: KI Entertainment, Unit 21 317-321 Woodpark Road, Smithfield, New South Wales 2164, Australia Tel: 0 800 850 777 Fax: +612 9604 3699 Email: sales@kientertainment.com.au

NIGERIA: FBFM, Helen Baugh House, 96 St Finbarr's College Road, Akoka, Lagos Tel: (+234) 01-7747429, 08075201777, 08186337699, 08154453905 Email: fbfm_1@yahoo.com

PHILIPPINES: OMF Literature Inc, 776 Boni Avenue, Mandaluyong City Tel: (02) 531 2183 Fax: (02) 531 1960 Email: gloadlaon@omflit.com

SINGAPORE: Alby Commercial Enterprises Pte Ltd, 95 Kallang Avenue #04-00, AIS Industrial Building, 339420 Tel: (+65) 629 27238 Fax: (+65) 629 27235 Email: marketing@alby.com.sg

SOUTH AFRICA: Life Media & Distribution, Unit 20, Tungesten Industrial Park, 7 C R Swart Drive, Strydompark 2125 Tel: (+27) 0117924277 Fax: (+27) 0117924512 Email: orders@lifemedia.co.za

SRI LANKA: Christombu Publications (Pvt) Ltd, Bartleet House, 65 Braybrooke Place, Colombo 2 Tel: (+941) 2421073/2447665 Email: christombupublications@gmail.com

USA: David C Cook Distribution Canada, PO Box 98, 55 Woodslee Avenue, Paris, Ontario N3L 3E5, Canada Tel: 1800 263 2664 Email: joy.kearley@davidccook.ca

CWR is a Registered Charity – Number 294387
CWR is a Limited Company registered in England – Registration Number 1990308